Lerner Wildlife Library

Animals of the DESERTS

written by Sylvia A. Johnson

illustrated by Alcuin C. Dornisch

Lerner Publications Company · Minneapolis, Minnesota

LIBRARY OF CONGRESS CATALOGING IN PUBLICATION DATA

Johnson, Sylvia A.
  Animals of the deserts.

  (Lerner Wildlife Library)
  SUMMARY: Describes desert life and ten animals living in desert areas of the world: the kit fox, Arabian camel, caracal, gemsbok, roadrunner, onager, sidewinder, antelope jackrabbit, addax, and ringtail.

  1. Desert fauna—Juvenile literature. [1. Desert animals] I. Dornisch, Alcuin C. II. Title.

QL116.J63 1976   599'.09'0954   75-27754
ISBN 0-8225-1279-3

Manufactured in the United States of America

International Standard Book Number: 0-8225-1279-3
Library of Congress Catalog Card Number: 75-27754

4 5 6 7 8 9 10 90 89 88 87 86 85 84 83 82

Contents

Animals of the DESERTS

The desert of our imaginations is a bleak and lifeless land, scorched by the sun and swept by blowing wind and sand. But the real deserts of the world are not such empty, barren places. There is life in the desert, and color, and variety. There are flowering plants and thriving animals and even flowing streams in many of the world's deserts. The desert is a place of special beauty and an environment with its own unique characteristics and ways of life.

What are the characteristics that make the desert what it is? One of the most important is, of course, dryness—in scientific terms, a desert is an area that receives less than 10 inches (25 centimeters) of rainfall a year. Some of the world's deserts receive as little as half an inch of rain during an average year. And very often, this extreme dryness is accompanied by extreme heat; the lack of moisture in the desert air allows the sun's rays to penetrate the atmosphere and to heat the land to a greater extent than in humid areas. Thus, temperatures in many deserts often rise to 120 degrees F (49 degrees C) during a typical day.

Yet the desert is not always scorchingly hot. Desert nights are very cold, for the same reasons that the days are torrid. Because there is no protective layer of moisture in the air, the heat of the earth soon escapes back into the atmosphere when the sun sets. Temperatures may actually drop 50 degrees or more at night. And just as the desert is not always hot, so, too, it is not always bone-dry. At times there are great storms in the desert, and rain comes pouring down in torrents. When this happens, flash floods often occur, for the dry soil cannot quickly absorb the large quantities of water.

Raging floods, freezing temperatures—these are not things that we ordinarily associate with deserts. But they do exist, and they serve to prove that the desert is not the land of endless heat and drought that people usually imagine. The climate of the desert is one of extreme change, varying from heat to cold, from dryness to an excess of moisture. The individual deserts of the world vary, too, in their climates and in the characteristics of their soil and land formations. Some deserts, like the Gobi in Central Asia, have relatively high altitudes and thus are cooler than deserts like the Sahara and the Arabian, which are located at lower altitudes and are also closer to the Equator. The Arabian is a sandy desert, containing within its territory thousands of acres of rolling sand dunes. One-third of the Arabian desert is covered with sand, whereas the Sahara, much larger in size, is one-tenth sand and nine-tenths rock and gravel. The landscape of the North American desert is more varied, with jagged cliffs and deep valleys, salt flats and wind-carved hills.

Although the deserts of the world differ in their characteristics, the scarcity of water is the one factor that controls all desert environments. Because of this lack of water, green plants do not grow abundantly in desert areas. Yet even in the driest deserts, some vegetation can be found, and in many of the world's deserts, there is a surprising amount of plant life.

The plants that take root in desert soil are different from the plants that grow in milder climates. The harsh conditions under which they live have forced desert plants to develop specialized methods of growth and survival. When there is no water available, many desert plants become dormant, sinking into a state of inactivity and rest. Plants such as the ocotillo and the paloverde of the American desert shed their leaves during times of drought, so that precious moisture can be used to keep their roots and stems alive. Annual plants—those that develop, reproduce, and die during a single growing season—live through extended dry periods in the form of seeds buried in the soil, awaiting the moisture that will bring them to life.

When moisture is available, desert plants make use of it in many remarkable ways. Succulent plants like the cactus store water for future use in the spongy tissues of their stems and leaves. Other plants conserve water in underground storage bulbs, while still others send down long roots to tap the water deep beneath the desert soil. All the plants of the desert are prepared to take full advantage of the water that comes in the form of infrequent but heavy rainstorms. When the rains come, desert trees produce

Deserts of the World

bright green leaves overnight, and brilliant flowers appear amid the spiny thorns of cactus plants. Soaked by a heavy rain, desert annuals will burst into bloom, mature, produce new seeds, and die, all within a few short weeks.

Despite its harsh and demanding climate, the desert is able to support a great variety of plant life. Desert plants, in turn, make possible the existence of the community of desert animals. The animals of the desert, like all the living creatures of the world, depend upon green plants to supply the food that they need for life. Where plants are plentiful in the desert, animals will be found as well—insects that drink the nectar of desert flowers, birds and small mammals that eat the seeds of desert plants, reptiles and larger mammals that feed on the plant eaters. Like the sturdy desert plants, the animals of the desert have developed various methods of surviving the harshness of their environment. Amidst the heat and the dryness of the desert, these remarkable animals are able to live and thrive.

8

Kit Fox

When twilight falls on the deserts of North America, many animals leave their dens and move quietly and swiftly through the shadows. Among these silent prowlers of the desert night is the dainty little kit fox (*Vulpes velox*). No bigger than a large house cat, the kit fox is nevertheless a skillful and deadly hunter, preying on the small rodents and insects that share its environment. The animal's large, fur-lined ears enable it to find its prey easily amid the nighttime shadows. Each of these large ears can be moved independently so that the kit fox can listen for sounds coming from two different directions at the same time. Its hearing is very sharp, alert to the slightest rustle of sand or rattle of twigs in the silence of the night. When it hears a sound indicating the presence of prey, it hurries off to find a meal. The kit fox's hunting expeditions take place only during the sunless hours of the desert night. In the heat of the day, the little mammal finds shelter within its den, which is a long, narrow burrow dug deep into the cool soil beneath the desert floor. Like all the animals of the desert, the kit fox has learned to live its life in rhythm with the changes of its extreme environment.

Arabian Camel

Of all the animals that make their homes in the world's deserts, the camel is probably the best known. This sturdy, long-legged creature has been a companion to the human inhabitants of the deserts for thousands of years. At one time, many camels roamed wild, but almost all camels living today are tame animals that are owned by the desert people of Africa and Asia. The two-humped Bactrian camel (*Camelus bactrianus*) serves as a source of food and a means of transportation in the deserts of Central Asia; the one-humped Arabian camel (*Camelus dromedarius*) earns its living in the deserts of North Africa and the Middle East. (The animal pictured here is an Arabian camel.) Both the Arabian and the Bactrian camel have many characteristics that make them perfectly suited for desert life, but perhaps their most fascinating features are their famous humps. A camel's hump is not a

storage place for water, as many people think, but a supply of spare food. The hump is made up mostly of fat, and it can be used as a source of energy when other food is scarce. Because a camel carries its own food supply, it is able to survive for days or even weeks without the grasses and plants on which it usually feeds. The animal is also able to go without water for long periods at a time. Camels do not carry a spare supply of water with them, but their bodies can use small amounts of water very efficiently. When drinking water is scarce, a camel can survive by drawing on the water contained within the tissues of its body. It is possible for a camel to lose as much as a quarter of its body weight in this way and still be healthy and capable of work. Water is also conserved because a camel's body puts out very little water in the form of perspiration. Perspiration helps animals to maintain a normal body temperature in a hot environment, but a camel's body temperature can vary quite a bit without causing any problem. In all of these ways, a camel is able to make good use of the precious moisture that is so important to survival in the desert.

Caracal

Morgan Hill
Country School

The beautiful caracal (KAR-uh-kal) is a member of the cat family that makes its home in the desert regions of Asia and Africa. This attractive feline is a relative of the bobcat, a small, fierce cat that can be found in the deserts of North America. Both the caracal and the bobcat have short tails and large ears with tufts of hair on their tips. The caracal's ear tufts are particularly striking—long, black, and stiff, they give the animal a very distinctive appearance. Like the bobcat and all other wild cats, the caracal is a powerful hunter skilled at stalking and killing prey. Birds are a favorite food of the caracal, and the little predator is so quick and agile that it is able to jump six feet (1.8 meters) into the air in order to catch its airborne prey. The hunting skills of the caracal, like those of its distant relative the cheetah, have sometimes been put to use by human beings. The people of India have trained caracals as hunters, and the fierce cats have learned to capture prey for human masters. In the wild, however, the caracal has no master. Its enemies are few, and, like all cats, it leads a life of freedom and independence.

Gemsbok

The deserts of Africa are inhabited by several different kinds of antelopes, swift-moving animals with horns of all shapes and sizes. Some of the most beautiful of these antelopes are the oryxes, and the gemsbok (*Oryx gazella*) is probably the most spectacular member of the oryx family. The gemsbok's face and legs and the underside of its body are distinctively marked with streaks of black and white. The big antelope's horns are long (4 feet or 1.2 meters) and straight, with pointed tips and ridged surfaces. These sharp horns make dangerous weapons when a gemsbok is forced to defend itself against an enemy. If the animal is cornered and unable to flee, it will lower its head and stab at its attacker with its deadly horns. But the gemsbok cannot easily defend itself against the attack of the Bushmen, native people who share the antelope's home in the bleak Kalahari Desert of South Africa. These expert hunters use poison-tipped arrows to kill the gemsbok and other animals for food. The Bushmen are as much at the mercy of the Kalahari's harsh environment as are the nonhuman inhabitants of the desert. They must kill in order to eat, and the gemsbok must sometimes lose its life so that the human animals may survive.

Roadrunner

A long-legged bird that runs across the hot desert floor instead of flying through the cool upper air: that is the roadrunner (genus *Geococcyx*) of the North American deserts. This unusual desert animal has learned to rely on its legs and feet rather than its wings in pursuing prey or escaping from enemies. The roadrunner can fly if it has to, but the bird is clumsy and slow on the wing. On foot, however, it is graceful and speedy, capable of running as fast as 15 miles (24 kilometers) an hour. The road-runner does most of its running during the day, when the heat of the desert is most severe. It does not hide from the sun but in fact often spends the early morning hours sunbathing with its wings spread and its feathers puffed out. After its sun bath is finished, the roadrunner sets off to find something to eat. The bird will eat just about anything—cactus fruits, insects, mice, toads, snakes, lizards. The roadrunner is particularly fond of snakes and lizards; it kills these quick-moving reptiles by striking them with its large, hard beak. If a reptile is too large to be swallowed in one gulp, then the roadrunner simply lets part of the animal hang out of its mouth while it goes about its business. After the first course of its meal is digested, the bird swallows the second course and disposes of it as well.

Onager

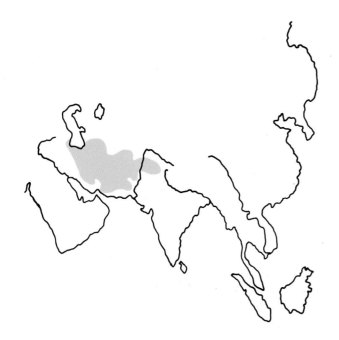

The onager (AHN-uh-jer), or Asiatic wild ass, is a member of the horse family that looks quite a bit like its close relative the domestic donkey. This curious animal has a history that extends back for thousands of years. Many people believe that the onager is the wild ass described in the Old Testament, "whose house [is] the wilderness, and the barren land his dwelling place. . . . The range of the mountains is his pasture, and he searches after every green thing" (Job 39:5-8). Even today, this is an accurate description of the onager and its way of life. The barren land in which the onager dwells is a mountainous desert region in west-central Asia. Vegetation is sparse in this area, and the onager must search far and wide in order to find the green plants on which it feeds. Like the camel, the onager has a remarkable ability to go without water for long periods of time. Onagers also share the camel's capacity for taking in enormous quantities of water when it *is* available. These sturdy animals seem very well suited to their difficult lives in the desert wilderness. Traveling in small herds led by a single stallion, onagers gallop endlessly over the dry hills of their homeland, seeking out the food and water that they need to stay alive.

Sidewinder

Several different kinds of rattlesnakes live in the deserts of North America. One of the most interesting of these poisonous snakes is the little sidewinder (*Crotalus cerastes*), a desert animal with an unusual method of locomotion. This snake's common name comes from its habit of "sidewinding" its way across the loose sand of the desert floor.

When the sidewinder crawls, it moves its body in a series of sideways curves that leave peculiar J-shaped tracks in the sand. Sidewinding is an efficient method of moving over loose, sliding sand that is also used by several snakes of the African deserts. American sidewinders do their sidewinding only during the cool hours of the desert night. The extreme heat of the day is deadly to these snakes, as it is to all reptiles, because the animals are unable to regulate their body temperatures. During the hottest hours of the day, the sidewinder rests quietly in the shade or buries itself in the sand. When night falls, the snake comes to life and glides away through the shadows, searching for the rodents, lizards, and other small animals on which it feeds. The sidewinder finds its prey with the aid of a special sense organ—a small pit on its head that reacts to the heat put out by the bodies of other animals. Following this trail of heat, the snake locates its victim and bites it with hollow fangs that inject venom and bring quick death.

The antelope jackrabbit (*Lepus alleni*) is a desert dweller with a rather mixed-up name. In the first place, this inhabitant of the North American deserts is not a true rabbit at all, but a hare, a larger and heavier member of the rabbit family. The antelope part of the jackrabbit's name is not quite accurate either. The animal is called an *antelope* jackrabbit because it shares a characteristic with the pronghorn, a horned mammal of the dry western grasslands that is often mistakenly referred to as an antelope. What the jackrabbit and the pronghorn have in common is the ability to "flash" the white hairs on their rumps by making these hairs stand erect. Both animals use this flash of white as a warning signal to other members of their species. Another interesting characteristic of the antelope jackrabbit, one not shared by the pronghorn, is the animal's amazingly long ears. As much as eight inches (20 centimeters) in length, these beautiful ears are so thin that when they are held erect, the sun shines through them, revealing the tiny blood vessels within the tissue. Some scientists think that the jackrabbit's ears help the animal to keep cool in the desert by passing out body heat through the blood vessels and into the air. It is definitely known that the huge ears are efficient in their primary function, hearing. At the slightest sound of a predator approaching quietly through the desert night, the antelope jackrabbit takes off with a bound, flattening its long ears against its back to keep them out of danger. Sometimes its race for life is successful; at other times, this plant-eater of the desert loses its life in order that a desert meat-eater may find food and survive.

Addax

The addax (AD-aks) is another species of antelope that lives in the deserts of Africa. Closely related to the African oryxes, the addax is a native of the vast Sahara, one of the largest and most barren deserts in the world. Addaxes make their homes deep in the desert, in areas of blowing sand and scarce water. The antelopes are able to live in this extreme environment because, like so many desert creatures, they can survive on very small amounts of water. When there is no water to drink, addaxes depend on the moisture contained in the green plants that they eat. In order to obtain the food they need, the animals will travel many miles to reach an area where vegetation can be found. Their broad, spreading hooves enable them to move swiftly over the shifting sand without sinking in. But however fast and skillfully the addax moves, it cannot escape the human inhabitants of the desert who use motor vehicles to pursue the beautiful antelope. These hunters, armed with powerful guns, kill the animal for its flesh or for its amazing twisted horns and sand-colored hide. As a result of this kind of slaughter, the addax is becoming increasingly rare. Even in the most remote areas of the great desert, the animal is not safe from people who use the inventions of modern civilization to destroy a part of natural life.

Ringtail

The bright-eyed ringtail (*Bassariscus astutus*) is a small desert animal that belongs to the raccoon family. Its home is in the deserts of the United States and Mexico, and, like so many desert dwellers, it is a creature of the night. After sleeping soundly all day, the ringtail leaves its den at dusk and begins hunting for food—berries, lizards, insects, mice. Mice are the ringtail's favorite food, and the little mammal is an expert at catching this quick-moving prey. In fact, ringtails have frequently aided human inhabitants of the desert by catching and eating the mice that live near desert cabins or camps. In the past, miners and prospectors in the American desert often kept a tame ringtail as a mouse catcher and a pet. This practice gave the ringtail one of its many nicknames—the miner's cat. Another common name for the ringtail is cacomistle (KAK-uh-miss-uhl), a word that originated among the Aztec Indians of Mexico, who were familiar with the animal long before Europeans came to the deserts of the New World. Today, the people of Mexico still use this ancient name for the little desert creature. North Americans call the animal "ringtail" in honor of the conspicuous black-and-white stripes that form rings around its long, fluffy tail. Whatever its name, the ringtail is one of the most attractive and appealing inhabitants of the American deserts.

Scale of Animal Sizes

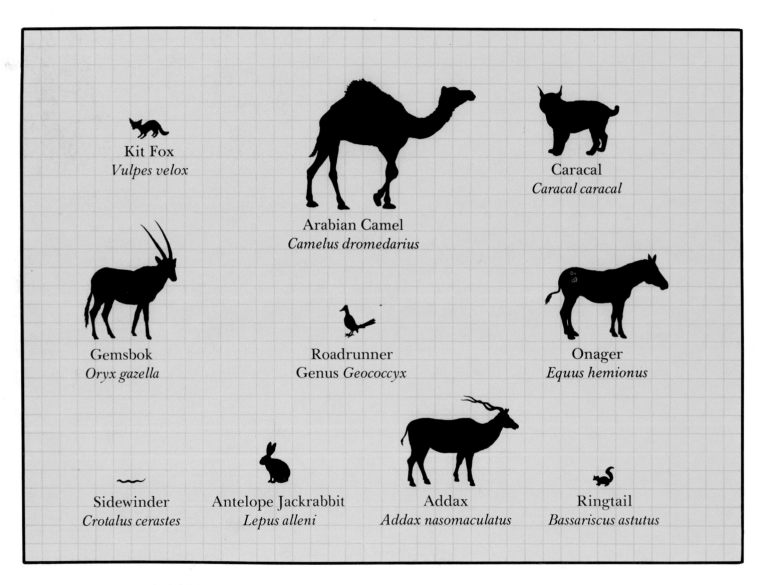

Kit Fox
Vulpes velox

Arabian Camel
Camelus dromedarius

Caracal
Caracal caracal

Gemsbok
Oryx gazella

Roadrunner
Genus *Geococcyx*

Onager
Equus hemionus

Sidewinder
Crotalus cerastes

Antelope Jackrabbit
Lepus alleni

Addax
Addax nasomaculatus

Ringtail
Bassariscus astutus

= 1 Foot   = 1 Meter   *Animals of the Deserts*